Enjoying the
PEAK DISTRICT

Enjoying the PEAK DISTRICT

ROLY SMITH

HALSGROVE

Published in
Partnership with the

First published in Great Britain in 2003

British Library Cataloguing-in-Publication Data
A CIP record for this title is available from the British Library

ISBN 1 84114 276 X

HALSGROVE

Halsgrove House
Lower Moor Way
Tiverton EX16 6SS
Tel: 01884 243242
Fax: 01884 243325
email: sales@halsgrove.com
website: www.halsgrove.com

Printed by D'Auria Industrie Grafiche Spa, Italy

CONTENTS

Wirksworth

FOREWORD

THE PEOPLE'S PARK

Welcome to *Enjoying the Peak District*, and I hope that this new publication will help you to do just that.

Over the years, the Peak District has been a wonderful recreational resource, being on the doorsteps of the huge conurbations of the cities of the industrial north which surround it. It has always been the most *accessible* of the National Parks, and our policies which support the use of public transport try to keep it that way, even for those of you who don't own a car.

National Parks are no longer the preserve of the élite middle class which were so instrumental in setting them up half a century ago. Indeed, it could be said that the Peak was never like that. Since the days of the Mass Trespassers seventy years ago, it has been the playground of people from all classes and ranks of society.

One of our major ambitions today is to continue to make it freely available to people of all classes of our modern, multi-racial society. Through initiatives such as the Mosaic Project, managed by the Council for National Parks, which aims to encourage people from ethnic communities to visit and enjoy the area, along with our updated *Access for All* booklet, which helps people with disabilities, whether they are blind, deaf, or bound to a wheelchair, we are working to make the Peak District available to everyone.

We don't believe that just because you come from a different ethnic background, or because you suffer from some kind of disability, that you should not be able to enjoy the Peak District just like everyone else.

The Peak has always been known as 'the People's Park,' and that's just the way we want to keep it.

Enjoy your visit.

Tony Hams
Chairman, Peak District
National Park Authority

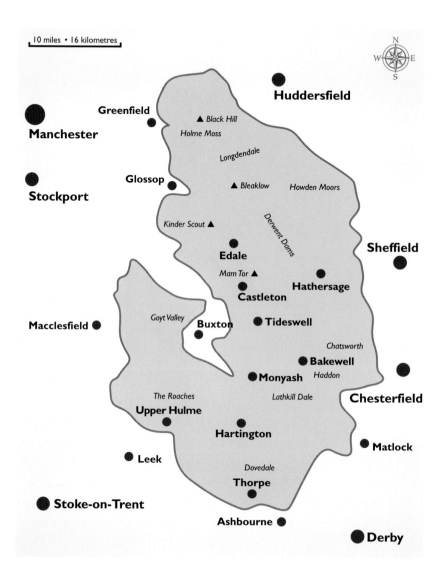

INTRODUCTION

FIRST AND LAST

The Peak District National Park was the first National Park in Britain – designated in April, 1951. Standing on the border between highland and lowland Britain, it represented the last piece of relatively unspoilt landscape left between the sprawling industrial cities of Manchester, Sheffield, the Potteries and West Yorkshire.

So in many ways, it was a National Park where it was most needed.

The Peak District's unique situation has been recognised not only by its National Park status, the highest possible designation for landscape protection, but also by a whole range of nature conservation designations. The same accident of geography has made the Peak a home to a unique community of plants and animals, some at their southernmost and others at their northernmost range (see At the Crossroads chapter).

Large parts of the Dark Peak moors, for example, are designated Special Areas of Conservation (SACs) and Special Protected Areas (SPAs) under European legislation because of their internationally important moorland habitats for birds such as the golden plover, peregrine falcon and merlin. There are over 60 Sites of Special Scientific Interest (SSSIs), and the Derbyshire Dales National Nature Reserve (NNR) covers 356ha of the White Peak's most beautiful, flower-rich limestone dales.

Industry

Despite its appearance in places as an untamed wilderness, this is a landscape which has been shaped and adapted by man over many centuries. The mineral wealth of the Peak has been exploited since the days of the Romans, who came here in search of lead, and for many centuries, the lead mining industry was part of an important dual economy for White Peak farmers.

Today, the waste that the lead miners discarded is in demand as a source of fluorspar, which is used in the chemical and steel industries, while other larger limestone quarries use the stone for road aggregates and chemical use. Smaller gritstone quarries still use the stone, as they traditionally have, for building and roofing material.

The water power of the great Peakland rivers such as the Derwent and Wye was utilised by Richard Arkwright in the first water-powered cotton mills in the world, at Cromford, now part of the Derwent Mills World Heritage Site. Plentiful, clean water supplies and the narrow Dark Peak valleys attracted the water engineers of the early twentieth century, and now over 50 reservoirs flood these valleys, creating another, not unattractive, landscape to be enjoyed by visitors.

Hartington village

Farming is still the major industry in the Peak, and meat and dairy products – tasty hill-farmed lamb and specialist cheeses such as Hartington's unique Stilton, for example – are now marketed at specialist outlets and farmers' markets.

Outdoor pursuits

It is nearly sixty years since Prof. C.E.M. Joad stated that in his day 'hiking had replaced beer as the shortest cut out of Manchester'. Writing in his *The Untutored Townsman's Invasion of the Country* in 1946, he described what he called 'the second industrial revolution' which had enabled townspeople to escape at weekends into the surrounding countryside for recreation.

That wholesale exodus still takes place today from the industrial towns and cities which surround the Peak, thanks to the 'third wave' of Joad's revolution, mass car ownership, and is aided by a good public transport network which brings visitors in by bus and train.

It is probably still true to say that on any given day, there are likely to be more people out walking, climbing, cycling or riding in the Peak District than in all the other hill areas of Britain put together. The Peak is blessed with a wonderful network of rights of way and ancient bridleways where you can admire the scenery at first hand.

Edale village

Other, more genteel, visitors came to the Peak from the eighteenth century, to enjoy the spa waters of Buxton and Matlock Bath, where hydropathic treatments such as those supplied by John Smedley at Matlock were once the fashion. Today, the health-giving, pure waters of the Peak are exported all over the world through the mineral waters obtained from Buxton, Ashbourne and Wildboarclough.

Heritage and culture

The great urban architecture of the Peak is concentrated in those spa towns, especially Buxton, which boasts a perfect Georgian heart, with highlights that include the magnificent Crescent, the dome of the Devonshire Hospital, and the Pavilion Gardens.

The great country houses of Chatsworth, Haddon, Lyme and Hardwick dominate the countryside in their landscaped parklands, while in the villages, smaller country houses like the ancient halls at Eyam and Tissington, still lord it over their communities. The Peak is also rich in fine country churches, good examples being those at Tideswell – the 'cathedral of the Peak' – Bakewell and Youlgreave.

Long before man settled in towns and villages, sacred sites dominated the landscape of the Peak District hills, as the enigmatic stone circles of Arbor Low, Stanton Moor and Eyam Moor illustrate. Other prehistoric sites are being discovered every year, such as the Neolithic enclosure on Gardom's Edge, indicating that the landscape was heavily populated and exploited up to 5000 years ago.

The Peak's historic past is remembered in local museums such as those at Buxton and Bakewell, which reflect a traditional way of life that is being maintained by local crafts and regular weekly street markets. Also reflecting this past are the ancient customs, perhaps the best known being well dressings, which still take place in many Peak District villages during the summer months, to the delight of visitors.

And the cultural life of the Peak District continues to thrive in the shape of exciting arts festivals such as those held at Buxton, Bakewell and Wirksworth every year. The Peak District is a landscape which continues to surprise and delight the modern visitor – as it has for centuries.

FASCINATING FACTS

Did you know that the Peak District was:

- the first National Park in Britain, designated in 1951?

- the second most-visited National Park in the world, after Mt Fuji in Japan?

- the only British National Park to be awarded the Council of Europe's Diploma for protecting the area's natural and cultural heritage?

- the northernmost home of many southern species (such as the hobby and nettle-leaved bellflower) and…

- the southernmost home of many northern species (such as the mountain hare and cloudberry)?

- the only place in the world where Derbyshire feathermoss (*Thamnobryum angustifolium*) is found?

- the home of the World Toe-Wrestling Championships (held annually at Wetton in June)?

THE WHITE PEAK

The whole gift of the country is in its glens. The wide acreage of field or moor above is wholly without interest; it is only in the clefts of it, and the dingles, that the traveller finds his joy.

John Ruskin's typically emphatic opinion of the White Peak landscape in the nineteenth century might still be shared by the majority of today's visitors. But although Ruskin's 'glens and dingles,' such as Dovedale, Lathkill Dale, Bradford Dale and the Manifold Valley, are undoubtedly the scenic highlights, there is much more to the White Peak than that.

Dovedale

The area known as the White Peak extends from Ashbourne and the Matlocks in the south to Castleton and the Hope Valley in the north. Its western edge is marked by the beautiful Manifold Valley, and the east by the mighty River Derwent.

It gets its distinctive name from the underlying Carboniferous limestone bedrock, laid down 350 million years ago under a shallow tropical sea, when what we now know as the Peak District was considerably nearer to the Equator. This can be proved by a closer look at one of the drystone walls which cover the rolling plateau in a network of patiently constructed boundaries. A detailed inspection will show that each stone is made up of millions of fossils – sea lilies and tiny shellfish – which lived and died in the pea soup of that primordial ocean.

Detail of crinoid fossils in a limestone gatepost

On the outskirts of many White Peak villages, you will find a small, often now overgrown quarry, where the stone for the cottages and walls of the village was obtained. Some of these later developed into the massive limestone quarries of today, such as those found around Buxton and the cement works at Hope, still important local sources of employment. The flower-filled meadows of the White Peak are full of bumps and hollows, most of which were left behind by the generations of lead miners who doubled here as farmers for something like 200 years. The most impressive ruin they left behind is probably Magpie Mine, near Sheldon, a place full of history and ghosts.

That underlying geology has created another, usually unseen, landscape, where the porous limestone has led to the creation of an underground world of caves and

An aerial view of Magpie Mine

caverns, some of which can be enjoyed by visitors in the show caves of Castleton, Buxton, and Matlock. In addition to lead ore, minerals in the limestone also created the unique semi-precious gemstone known as Blue John, only found around Treak Cliff at Castleton. Underground mineral springs, first discovered by the Romans, also led to the creation of the elegant spa town of Buxton, and also to John Smedley's short-lived spa at Matlock.

The White Peak plateau averages about 1000 feet (300m) above the sea, so it can be a bleak place in winter. But in summer the sight of the bright green pastures encased in the white walls, most of which were built during the Enclosure Movements of the eighteenth and nineteenth centuries, is the lasting memory of the Peak District for many people.

Those spectacular dales were carved out relatively recently in the immense geological timescale. It was at the end of the last Ice Age, between 10,000 and 15,000 years ago, that they were created, as the glaciers finally melted and sent down mighty deluges of erosive meltwater across the plateau. It is hardly conceivable that the insignificant rivers which now run through the dales (and which often disappear

15

Minninglow

underground completely during the summer) could have created the magnificent rock architecture of crags and pinnacles which now grace them.

Occasionally, harder limestones were created on the edge of coral reefs, and these remain – such as Chrome and Parkhouse Hills in the Manifold Valley and Bunster and Thorpe Cloud in Dovedale – as some of the few real peaks which justify the name in the Peak District.

Most White Peak dales are narrow and intimate, threaded not by roads as in the broader dales of Yorkshire to the north, but only by footpaths or ancient tracks, which are so enticing to the walker. Many of the dales are now protected as nature reserves, such is their wealth of flora and fauna, and the most important form the Derbyshire Dales National Nature Reserve centred on Lathkill Dale, managed by English Nature as one of its flagship sites.

But what of the 'wide acreage of field and moor above', so summarily dismissed by Ruskin two centuries ago? The gently rolling White Peak plateau is the real treasure-house of prehistory in the Peak, where the first permanent settlers in the region, perhaps 5000 years ago, left reminders of their presence.

We know much more about how these people treated their dead, from the monuments they left behind, than how they actually lived. There are estimated to be more than 500 tumuli or burial mounds in the White Peak alone – and almost every one is known by the misleading name of 'low'. The word comes from the Old English *hlaw* for a hill or mound, and paradoxically, most are found on the highest points in the landscape. Most date from the Bronze Age, and were systematically but not entirely scientifically 'excavated' by Victorian antiquaries, one of whom was Thomas Bateman of Middleton-by-Youlgreave.

You can see many of these lows as little pimples on top of the surrounding hills as you stand on the massive embankments of enigmatic Arbor Low, a Neolithic henge monument and stone circle near Middleton, which is sometimes known as 'the Stonehenge of the North'. Dating from the same period as its better-known counterpart in Wiltshire, Arbor Low's once standing stones are all more or less lying flat, and a Bronze Age burial mound was superimposed on the eastern rim of its embankment some 3000 years after its original construction.

THE WALLS WALK SLOWLY

Perhaps the most lasting impression of the White Peak left with visitors, especially those coming from the south, is the network of drystone walls which enmesh the landscape, up hill and down dale. It has been estimated that there are over 26,000 miles of drystone walls in the White Peak alone. That's equivalent to a wall which would more than encircle the Earth at the Equator!

Most were constructed during the Enclosure Movement of the eighteenth and nineteenth centuries, as landowners sought to enclose and tame the wild moorlands which then marked the Peak. Gangs of men marked out and built the walls using the abundant natural stone and, if the tale is true, never putting down a stone which had been picked up until they had found a home for it in the wall.

Most of these walls are around 200–300 years old, but recent archaeological dating techniques has shown that some of the limestone walls in the White Peak may go back to Roman times, and are an astonishing 2000 years old.

Drystone walls at Wardlow

Lathkill Dale

THE DARK PEAK

It is a wild, vast place, far from the ways of men, who here are the most occasional of creatures, and all its notes have the sadness of great spaces – of the mountains, moors and seas. And yet it does one good to escape to this upland, age-long solitude, where the primeval world is felt to be a mighty fact, linked on to us.

John Derry's description of the scene on Back Tor, Derwent Edge, was written nearly a century ago, but as a vivid expression of the sense of freedom imparted by the Dark Peak moors, it has scarcely been bettered. These desolate peat moors have attracted wilderness lovers for many years, and their wide open spaces offered the perfect antidote to the citizens of the surrounding towns and cities who had spent their workaday weeks in grim and smoky factories, mills and steelworks.

For the purposes of this book, the Dark Peak encompasses all the high moorland north from Edale, including Kinder Scout, Bleaklow and Black Hill, to Holmfirth. It is bordered to the west by the former textile towns of Glossop and Chapel-en-le-Frith, to the south down to the moorlands around Buxton, and to the east by the Howden and Derwent moors.

As with the White Peak to the south, the name reflects the sombre colour of the vegetation and the rocks, in this case millstone grit, which underlie the blanket peatbogs on the highest points. No peaks here, either, as the highest ground of Kinder and Bleaklow consists of barren plateaux of peat moorland, criss-crossed by a maze of drainage channels known as 'groughs.' They were once described as 'Britain's only true desert,' but they are only a desert in the sense that little lives or grows there. This is a cold and soggy, sub-Arctic wilderness, sharing the same latitude as Siberia or Labrador.

The hard, abrasive gritstone was laid down over the limestones when a gigantic river flowing from the north covered the former tropical sea with tons of gritty sediment, eventually to be petrified into the rocks we see today. Later aeons of wind, frost and rain carved the harder elements into the exotically-shaped tors which edge the moors at places like the Woolpacks on the southern edge of Kinder Scout. The few towns and villages, Glossop, Chapel, Edale and Holmfirth and the like, shelter in the lee of

Gritstone sheep

these forbidding moors, for although the moorland streams provided power for the mills which were built in the valleys during the Industrial Revolution, the moors were always kept at arm's length.

Apart from the users of the few ancient packhorse trails which crossed them, the moors were only frequented by the hardy hill farmers and shepherds, to gather their ubiquitous sheep. Local breeds such as the Derbyshire Gritstone and Whitefaced Woodland somehow manage to find enough to eat in the peaty wilderness.

Here the effects of ancient clearance of woodland, soils poor in nutrients, moorland fires and the altitude have combined with years of overgrazing to create a barren landscape which was once memorably described as 'land at the end of its tether'. These vast areas of moorland have traditionally been managed for just two creatures, the moorland sheep and red grouse. The latter need heather for almost every aspect of their lives (see box), and so most of the heather moorland has been created and managed specifically for this bird, with the shooting season in mind, opening on 'the Glorious Twelfth' of August each year.

Modern management and restoration techniques, along with schemes such as the National Park Authority's *Moors for the Future* project, are combining to slowly

Woolpacks, Kinder Scout

Fairbrook, Kinder Scout

reverse the trend of moorland deterioration, and heather can now be seen growing in places like Kinder Scout where it has not been seen for many years.

Important trails have always crossed the highest and wildest of the Dark Peak moors, such as the Cut Gate Track linking Langsett and the Derwent Valley, and Doctor's Gate, along the line of a former Roman road, between Glossop and the Derwent. These former packhorse routes eventually developed into roads such as the Snake Pass, one of the highest roads in England, which crosses between Kinder and Bleaklow at over 1600 feet (500m) linking Sheffield and Glossop. Further north, Longdendale runs up to the Woodhead Pass and links Stocksbridge and Manchester, and was crossed by a Victorian railway which has now been converted to the Longdendale Trail, part of the TransPennine Trail.

The other important land use of the Dark Peak moors is for water collection. The deep valleys of the Dark Peak have been utilised for the last hundred years by the construction of dams and creation of over 50 reservoirs, notably in the Upper Derwent and Longdendale valleys, which feed clean water to the homes and factories of the neighbouring cities and towns.

Ramshaw Rocks

GLORIOUS GROUSE

One of the great sights of the Dark Peak comes in late summer when the purple-hued heather transforms the moorland into swathes of brilliant colour.

Just as the sheep have shaped the apparent wilderness of the peat moors, so the red grouse have shaped the acres of heather moorland which thrive on the drier, lower areas of the Dark Peak.

This plump, furry-footed game bird which is exclusive to Britain requires healthy heather for every stage of its development. It needs older, wiry heather to roost and breed in and the younger shoots of new heather to eat, in addition to a good supply of craneflies (or daddy longlegs) for its newborn chicks.

So many of the heather moors are carefully managed by owners to encourage good flocks of red grouse, which are shot by regulated parties after the 'Glorious Twelfth' of August, through to the end of the year.

Red grouse

THE DERWENT VALLEY

...for the Derwent is a frightful creature when the hills load her current with water; I say, we kept our distance, and contented ourselves with hearing the roaring of its waters...

Daniel Defoe's description of 'that fury of a river called the Derwent' comes from his *Tour thro' the Whole Island of Great Britain*, published in 1742. In the same book, he also commented on 'a Curiosity of a very extraordinary nature, and the only one of its kind in England' which he had recently witnessed taking place on its banks.

He was referring to the new textile mills which had sprung up to harness the tremendous power of the Peak District's major river. Pioneers such as Richard Arkwright at Cromford, Jedediah Strutt at Belper and George Sorocold at Derby, were the first to introduce a factory system in the world – and therefore could justly be nominated as among the founders of the Industrial Revolution.

Howden Dam, Upper Derwent

Fifteen miles of the Derwent Valley from Derby to Cromford and Matlock Bath was recently awarded World Heritage Site status by UNESCO, in recognition of its importance as the birthplace of the factory system and the site of the first commercial use of water to power textile mills.

Many of these mills can still be seen along the Derwent today, and Arkwright's first sites in Mill Lane are being restored. The red-brick Georgian façade of Masson Mill on the A6 Derby Road now houses a fashionable shopping outlet, where visitors can still see a working textile museum on the lower floor. The whole fascinating story of the industrialisation of the Derwent Valley is told at the Derwent Valley Visitor Centre in another mill, North Mill, at Belper.

The River Derwent rises high among the peat bogs on the Dark Peak moors just below the summit of Bleaklow, and in the course of its 20 miles running down the eastern side of the Peak District, it largely defines the surrounding landscape. To the west, the land slopes up through the dales to the pastures of the White Peak plateau, while its eastern boundary is more sharply defined by abrupt cliffs of gritstone, known as 'the Eastern Edges', which frown down over the river and its associated villages.

These sharp, steep crags of grey rock run almost continuously for some 12 miles down the eastern side of the Peak from Howden Edge past Derwent Edge, Stanage Edge, Froggatt Edge, Curbar Edge and Baslow and Birchen's Edge until they peter out on the moors above Matlock.

Today, they are the haunt of rock-climbers and hang-gliders, but in the past, like so many other Peak District landscapes, they were the sites of industry. Remains of this can still be found among the bracken and birch trees below the edges, where piles of discarded circular millstones lie in neat rows awaiting the buyers who never came. The industry, based at Hathersage and Froggatt and other villages, collapsed when cheaper imports from the Continent flooded the market.

Despite its reputation for ferocity, even the upper reaches of the mighty Derwent have to some extent been tamed by man. Not far below the boggy summit of Bleaklow, the moorland landscape has been transformed into what has been called the Peak District's Lake District. Three huge dams were constructed before the First and Second World Wars to impound the waters of the Derwent and create the enormous Howden, Derwent and Ladybower reservoirs which provided the fast-growing

Stanage Edge

industrial cities of Derby, Nottingham, Sheffield and Leicester with clean drinking water. The reservoirs are surrounded by vast coniferous forests originally planted to protect water purity, but which are now being gradually replaced by native trees.

'The Derwent Dams' as they are affectionately known, are now popular places for recreation for millions of visitors, who are managed by a unique and award-winning partnership between the water company, the National Park, the National Trust, and representatives from local district and parish councils.

The broad, pleasantly-wooded shale valley of the Derwent, and the Wye which takes a parallel course to the west, were chosen by the great landowners of the past as the places to build their grand houses. So in the landscaped parklands of Chatsworth, home of the Duke of Devonshire, and Haddon Hall, Derbyshire home of the Duke of Rutland, yet another, quite different, landscape is revealed.

Defoe memorably described Chatsworth as 'a palace for a prince' and marvelled that 'any man who had a genius suitable to so magnificent a design … would build it in such a place where the mountains insult the clouds…' Modern visitors still wonder at the foresight of Lancelot 'Capability' Brown, who two centuries ago diverted the Derwent and created the settled, harmonious landscape they come to admire today.

Grindleford

The villages of the Derwent Valley are almost all on the river and each have their ancient stone bridges providing safe crossings of that 'furious' river, and mills which once harnessed its power and now, in many cases, have been converted into luxurious living accommodation. The main settlements, apart from the Matlocks, Cromford and Bakewell, are at Bamford, Hathersage (legendary home of Robin Hood's faithful lieutenant, Little John), Grindleford, Baslow and Rowsley.

TALES OF TIN TOWN

When the two earliest Derwent Dams were being constructed, between 1901 and 1916, a temporary village – locally known as 'Tin Town' because of the corrugated iron used in its walls – was created for a population of nearly 1000, comprising the navvies and their families.

This short-lived community of Birchinlee was almost completely self-contained, with a recreation hall, canteen (pub), hospital, shops and school. The village had its own football teams, minister and policemen, and was an early and rare example of the concern which the constructors of the dams, the Derwent Valley Water Board, had for the welfare of its temporary employees.

Tin Town, which stood on the western shores of the present Derwent Reservoir for fifteen short years, is now just a memory, lost in the trees which blanket the reservoir.

Southwest Peak

Here are also vast Rocks which surprise with Admiration, called the Henclouds and Leek Roches. They are of so great a Height and afford such stupendous Prospects that one could hardly believe they were anywhere to be found but in Picture.

Dr Robert Plot, in his *Natural History of Staffordshire* published in 1686, was one of the first to recognise and record the astonishing landscapes of the Roaches and Hen Cloud, which pierce the skyline so dramatically as the motorist enters the Peak District on the A53 from Leek towards Buxton.

The moorlands of the southwest are the secret, hidden gem of the Peak District, often described as its 'Wild West'. From these rugged western heights, as Dr Plot pointed out three centuries ago, the views extend for miles across the broad green Cheshire Plain to the Tittesworth Reservoir and, on a clear day, to the distant silver glint of the River Mersey, reflecting the setting sun.

View near Shutlingsloe

The Roaches

Today the Roaches are popular with rock-climbers and hang-gliders as well as walkers, for whom the stroll along the crest of the escarpment past the mysterious Doxey Pool, one of few true mountain tarns to be found in the area, is one of the finest promenades in the Peak District.

Behind the Roaches and Ramshaw Rocks, a folded landscape of secret valleys, dark woods and wild moorland, rich in myths and folklore, lies hidden from the view of all but the most determined explorer. The southwest Peak is an area quite different and apart from the rest of the district, where ancient legends and customs still pervade the atmosphere like the mists which often wreathe the rocks.

In places like the secluded cleft of Lud's Church, tucked away in the depths of Back Forest to the north of the Roaches, the past is felt to be very close. And on a damp, autumnal day, the identification of the 30-feet deep fissure as the Green Chapel of the fourteenth century medieval alliterative poem *Sir Gawain and the Green Knight* seems entirely possible. Legend has it that the place was named after Walter de Ludank, a follower of the protestant Wycliffe, who held his illicit services here, far from the prying eyes of the establishment, until his daughter was accidentally shot by raiding soldiers.

And at Three Shires Head, where the counties of Derbyshire, Staffordshire and Cheshire meet at a tiny packhorse bridge crossing the infant River Dane in the heart of the moorlands, that feeling of being on the edge of things, remote from the rest of the world, is felt most strongly. Here in the bad old days, bare-knuckle prizefighters would meet for their illegal contests and if the authorities turned up, they would just step over into the next county to claim sanctuary. Up on the moors above, 'flash' or counterfeit money was minted at the village of Flash, at over 1500 feet, the highest in England.

Not far away is the tiny hamlet of Macclesfield Forest, once at the heart of Ranulf, Earl of Chester's royal hunting preserve in the Middle Ages, and now largely cloaked in the monotonous conifers planted after the First World War. The small, plain chapel here is still the scene of an annual rushbearing ceremony, where rushes are laid in the aisles for carpeting, just as they were in many village churches in days gone by. It is typical of the western moors that this ancient custom still takes place in this secluded spot every August.

Further north, the Goyt Valley represents the Dark Peak in microcosm. Surrounded by tawny moorland and deep coniferous forests, the deep valley has been

Goyt Valley

successively flooded by the reservoirs of Errwood and Fernilee. The hamlets of Goyt's Bridge and Errwood disappeared under the rising waters, and another victim was the Victorian Italianate mansion of Errwood Hall, home of the wealthy Grimshawe family, which was deliberately dismantled by the waterworks engineers in the interests of water purity.

Today, only the stark ruins of the hall remain deep in the forest, surrounded by acres of rhododendrons and azaleas brought back by the family from their frequent trips abroad in their private yacht. It remains a sad, melancholy place.

Further north, the Legh family's Palladian mansion of Lyme Park doubled as Pemberley in the recent TV adaptation of Jane Austen's *Pride and Prejudice*. It stands on the edge of Stockport, surrounded by moorland and the Peak's largest and wildest herd of red deer.

Settlements are few and far between on these western moors, and villages such as Kettleshulme, Wildboarclough, Warslow and Wetton are isolated, independent communities which often reflect their spartan surroundings. Their names often give

The former Crag Mill and Post Office at Wildboarclough

away the names of their founders, in the case of Kettleshulme, a Danish settler called Ketil. Hulme End, at the head of the Manifold Valley, has similar Scandinavian roots, while Cleulow Cross, standing in a windy plantation near the Buxton–Congleton road, is one of the finest Anglo-Scandinavian cross shafts in the Peak.

Most activity is centred on the former silk town of Leek, the capital of these moorlands which clustered around its cobbled market-place, somehow manages to give the air of a Lancashire cotton town. During the eighteenth and nineteenth centuries, several mills produced fine-quality silk cloth, some designed by William Morris and his Arts & Crafts followers. Here too the father of Britain's canals, James Brindley, was first apprenticed and learned his craft at a local water-mill, now a museum.

The clock tower in Leek market-place

South of Leek lies the lovely, secluded vale of the Churnet Valley, a well-wooded RSPB reserve, where the North Staffordshire Steam Railway still runs trains, and the Caldon Canal takes narrow boats past the Cheddleton Flint Mill, once used for the grinding of flint to be used in the nearby Potteries for china manufacture.

THE ART OF THE WALLER

A selection of some of the terms used in Peakland drystone walling:

Coping or cap stones – the upright stones that cap the top of the wall, sometimes known as 'buck and doe' stones

Through stones – strengthening stones which pass through the wall, sometimes used as a step-over stile

Squeezer stile – large upright stones too narrow for stock to pass through, used as a stile on a footpath

Cripple hole – a low hole in a wall which allows sheep but not cattle to pass through

Fillers – the smaller stones which are used to fill in the gap between the two faces of the wall

Footings – the large, flat foundation stones of a wall

Drystone waller

At the Crossroads

It has been a long accepted fact that the Peak District stands at the crossroads of Britain. With one foot in the bleak hills and moors of highland Britain and the other in the softer meadows and woodlands of the lowlands, the Peak offers a fascinating mix of habitats within a small, self-contained area.

So here we find northern types, such as crowberry, cloudberry, ring ouzel and mountain hare near their southernmost limit; while southern species, such as ivy-leaved bellflower, stemless thistle and hobby, are found here close to their northern extent. It truly is a naturalist's paradise.

Cloudberry

White Peak

The limestone dales of the White Peak have always provided the wildlife showplaces of the Peak, and many of the most important are now protected by English Nature as part of the Derbyshire Dales National Nature Reserve. Many other areas are protected as Sites of Special Scientific Interest (SSSIs).

A visit to one of the dales in spring or early summer is a pleasurable assault on all the naturalist's senses. The lime-rich soil encourages a wealth of herbs and wild flowers – up to 54 species per square metre in some parts – and they are famous for their extensive displays of early purple orchids, cowslips and rock rose. In other places, nationally rare species such as Jacob's ladder and Nottingham catchfly bloom in profusion, filling the air with their delicate scents.

Up on the limestone plateau, another transformation is taking place. For many years, farmers were encouraged to create monocultures of short-term leys sown with ryegrass for their cattle and sheep. This was disastrous for wildlife, especially for insects, and for waders such as the curlew and lapwing, which found nowhere to feed or breed successfully. More enlightened policies which have rewarded farmers to sensitively manage the old-fashioned wild flower and herb-rich meadows of the past have been followed by the National Park Authority and English Nature, backed by the government. The result is that today the loss of flower-rich grasslands is being gradually slowed down and, in a handful of places, even reversed. Grants for the upkeep of the old drystone walls also have the dual effect of retaining these important landscape features, and providing habitats and breeding spaces for animals such as weasels and little owls.

Dipper

The famous ash woods of Dovedale and Lathkill Dale are full of glorious bird-song as migrant species return to nest and breed, while the crystal-clear waters of the rivers also burst with new life. Perhaps the most characteristic bird of the White Peak rivers is the white-bibbed dipper, bobbing and bowing like a polite waiter on any prominent mid-stream rock, before embarking on its remarkable underwater search for food.

Dark Peak

Botanist and journalist John Hillaby's assessment of the Dark Peak moors in his *Journey through Britain* was pretty damning. 'From the botanical point of view,' he wrote, 'they are examples of land at the end of its tether. All the life has been drained off or burnt out, leaving behind only the acid peat. You can find nothing like them anywhere else in Europe.'

But when he walked through the Peak in the late 1960s, the erosion of the peat was at its worst, and nothing much was being done about it. In those days, a walk across Kinder was, as Hillaby described, 'extraordinarily depressing', the only sound being the faint cheep of meadow pipits 'like the last ticks of a clock that has almost run down'.

Today, more heather and other moorland plants such as bilberry and cloudberry can be seen on these moors than has been seen there for forty years. The reason is that the Kinder plateau is now being sympathetically managed for wildlife by its owners, the National Trust. Here and in many other moorland areas, owners are being encouraged by initiatives such as the *Moors for the Future* project, and their designations as Environmentally Sensitive Areas, Special Protected Areas for birdlife, and Special Area of Conservation for other wildlife habitats. As the effects of years of overgrazing have been realised, owners are being encouraged by grants to reduce the number of sheep and have wildlife habitats in mind as they manage their land.

Today, more extensive and better quality habitats are sustaining an increasing wildlife population on Kinder Scout, Bleaklow and the other Dark Peak moorlands, giving a much more secure future home to species such as the golden plover, peregrine falcon and merlin. And the glorious, purple-hued heather is regaining its hold to delight visitors and naturalists alike. Originally managed purely for the benefit of the red grouse, heather moorland is now seen as an important habitat for many other associated species, including protected predators such as the goshawk and peregrine.

A famous population of handsome pied flycatchers regularly returns to haunt the remnant sessile oak woods which cloak the clough at Padley Gorge, near Grindleford, and other native Dark Peak oak woods can be seen at Ladybower in the Upper Derwent Valley.

Larger, more spectacular, animals include Britain's biggest land mammal, the red deer, which grace the parklands of Chatsworth and Lyme alongside their more common fallow cousins, while the wild moorlands of Staffordshire once supported a breeding population of red-necked wallabies, descended from some released from a private collection during the Second World War.

RARER THAN THE TIGER

The tiny and insignificant Derbyshire feather moss (*Thamnobryum angusti-folium*) is rarer, in its humble way, than the tiger. This bryophyte (moss) remnant from the last Ice Age is found under a tumbling waterfall in a secluded White Peak dale – and nowhere else in the world.

Other wildlife rarities of the White Peak include the bright blue flowers of Jacob's ladder and the delicate Nottingham catchfly; and quartering the moorland skies of the Dark Peak can be seen the hen harrier, goshawk and spangle-backed golden plover.

Jacob's ladder

A PEAKLAND TIMELINE

10,000–8000 years ago — Palaeolithic (Old Stone) Age

The first hunter-gathers move onto the Peak District moors, following the retreat of the Ice Age glaciers. Earliest evidence of them is found in caves such as Thor's Fissure and Ossum's Cave in the Manifold Valley, and at Creswell Crags on the eastern edge of the area.

8000–5000 years ago — Mesolithic (Middle Stone) Age

Tiny slivers of flint known as microliths, sometimes uncovered in the peat of the Dark Peak moors, provide the only evidence of Mesolithic hunter-gatherers who hunted on these then tree-covered uplands for game.

5000–4000 years ago — Neolithic (New Stone) Age

The first farmers arrive, living in settlements such as that excavated at Lismore Fields, Buxton. They leave behind field systems and ritual monuments, such as the Arbor Low henge near Youlgreave and the Bull Ring at Dove Holes, as well as chambered tombs such as Minninglow and Five Wells, Taddington.

4000–3000 years ago — Bronze Age

The 500 tumuli or burial mounds in the White Peak, usually marked on the map as 'lows', provide evidence of the burial of chieftains, mainly dating from the Bronze Age. They leave behind distinctive cremation pottery, hut circles, field systems and ritual monuments, such as the Nine Ladies stone circle on Stanton Moor.

3000–2000 years ago — Iron Age

The age of the hill-forts, with fine examples at Mam Tor at the head of the Hope Valley, and Fin Cop, overlooking Monsal Dale. Hut circles inside indicate that the 'forts' were not always defensive, but probably used as summer dwelling places.

Aerial view of Arbor Low

Five Wells chambered tomb near Taddington

2000 years ago   Romans

The Romans probably arrive in the Peak District in the late 70sAD and establish forts at Navio near Brough and Melandra near Glossop, mainly to protect their lead mining interests. Buxton's civil settlement of *Aquae Arnemetiae* is based on the warm mineral springs in the town. The first roads and farmsteads are set up.

2000–1000 years ago   Dark Ages

First mention, in the *Tribal Hidage*, of the Pecsaetean or 'Dwellers of the Peak', when the Peak was part of Mercia. Christianity comes to the Peak, and Anglo-Saxon preaching crosses can still be seen in the churches at Bakewell, Eyam, Hope and Bradbourne. The first villages are established.

1000–1200AD   Normans

The first castles – of earthwork, 'motte and bailey' construction – are built at Bradfield, Bakewell and Pilsbury, followed by more substantial structures at Castleton, Bolsover and Duffield. The first manor houses and churches are built in the villages, and the Royal Forest of the Peak is established for hunting purposes.

1200–1400   Middle Ages

Markets are set up in the major villages, and fine churches such as those at Tideswell and Youlgreave are built on the wealth won from the dual economies of lead mining and farming. The extent of cultivated land is shown by the narrow strip fields at places like Chelmorton, and the acres of ridge and furrow and lynchets still seen in the White Peak landscape. Larger manors, such as Haddon Hall, are rebuilt.

1400–1700   Tudors and Stuarts

The age of the large landowners and the creation of the large country houses, estates and landscaped parklands of Chatsworth, Haddon and Lyme Hall by the Cavendish, Manners and Legh families. Plague strikes the village of Eyam in 1665–66, and the villagers impose a quarantine to stop it spreading. The first roads and turnpikes are created and the first travellers appear, but farming and lead mining remain the dominant local industries.

1700–1850   Industrial Revolution

Richard Arkwright chooses the soughs (drainage tunnels from lead mines) and streams feeding into the River Derwent at Cromford for his first commercial water-powered cotton mill. Other mills and factories follow at New Mills, Glossop, Leek

Pilsbury Castle

and Macclesfield, while new turnpike roads and the first railways appear. Landowners enclose much of the landscape in a network of drystone walls. The first tourists arrive by the new transport systems and better roads, and the 5th Duke of Devonshire develops Buxton as a spa.

1850–1900 Victorian Britain

The Railway Age dawns, and new routes start to cross the forbidding landscape of the Peak, such as the Midland line through the Wye Valley, the Woodhead across Longdendale, and the Hope Valley line. At the same time, tourism is boosted by the creation by John Smedley of a health spa at Matlock to match that at Buxton.

1900–1950 Modern Britain

Major engineering works create the Derwent Dams and the Longdendale Reservoirs, among 50 other reservoirs in the Peak, as the new industrialists and cities surrounding the Peak District realise the water-gathering potential of the area. The fast-expanding populations of the cities around use bus and train to reach the Peak District for their recreation, and calls for greater access to the moors culminate in the Mass Trespass on Kinder Scout in 1932. The Peak District National Park – the first in Britain – is designated in 1951.

ROYAL FORESTS OF THE PEAK

The Royal Forest of the Peak, which covered about 40 square miles between the valleys of the Wye and Etherow, was set up so that Norman kings could enjoy uninhibited hunting of deer, wild boar and wolves. As a protected area, it could be seen as the forerunner of the modern National Park, though the penalties for poaching were somewhat stricter than those of today. The Forest was administered from William Peverel's castle at Castleton with other important centres at Peak Forest and Chapel-en-le-Frith ('the chapel in the forest'). Macclesfield Forest in the west of the Peak was another royal forest, administered by Ranulph, Earl of Chester.

SOME KEY HISTORICAL FIGURES

Dark Ages: Edward the Elder, son of Alfred the Great, who in AD 920 built a 'burh' near Bakewell where he was recognised as 'father and lord' by other British kings.

Norman: William Peveril, illegitimate son of William the Conqueror, builder of Peveril Castle, Castleton and governor of the Royal Forest of the Peak.

Middle Ages: Richard de Vernon, builder of the first fortified Haddon Hall and ancestor of Sir George Vernon (d.1567), the so-called 'King of the Peak'.

Tudors and Stuarts: Elizabeth, or Bess of Hardwick, builder of Hardwick Hall and the original Chatsworth, and Bishop Robert Pursglove of Tideswell, who served in high office under Henry VIII, Edward VI, Mary Tudor and Elizabeth I.

Industrial Revolution: Richard Arkwright, Preston-born barber and wig maker, who built the world's first water-powered cotton mill and model factory village at Cromford in 1771, and James Brindley, Tunstead-born 'father' of the canal system.

Victorian: Joseph Paxton, head gardener at Chatsworth, who designed the Great Conservatory and later London's Crystal Palace for the Great Exhibition of 1851, and Thomas Bateman, pioneering archaeologist, from Middleton-by-Youlgreave.

Modern: Benny Rothman, Manchester-based leader of the Mass Trespass on Kinder Scout in 1932, which paved the way for National Parks and access to the countryside legislation.

Peveril Castle

CULTURE AND CUSTOMS

In such a remote area as the Peak District, customs and traditions tend to be protected and sustained by the isolated communities which faithfully honour them, year in and year out. And in the Peak's deepest dales and on its highest moors, myths and legends are remembered and recalled more frequently than in the surrounding lowlands, as the time-old tales are faithfully passed on from generation to generation.

But the Peak is also a stronghold for many cultural activities, and festivals like the annual Buxton Festival of Music and the Arts, centred on its ornate Opera House, attract performers and visitors from all over Britain and the rest of the world. More local arts festivals are springing up every year, such as at Bakewell and Wirksworth, and the Peak provides a popular backdrop to many film and TV dramas, ranging from *Last of the Summer Wine* based at Holmfirth, to *Peak Practice* in the Longnor area, *Pride and Prejudice* at Lyme Park, and the countless historical film dramas which have utilised the mellow, medieval walls of Haddon Hall, near Bakewell, as an authentic filmset.

Many writers, from Izaak Walton and Daniel Defoe to Lord Byron, John Ruskin and Alison Uttley, have found inspiration in the landscapes of the Peak District, Byron famously claiming 'there are things in Derbyshire as noble as in Greece or Switzerland.'

Perhaps the most famous of the Peak District's customs is that of well dressing, giving thanks for the precious gift of water, especially on the fast-draining limestone White Peak plateau. In fact, more village well dressings take place today than have ever been seen, as incomers are caught up with and intrigued by this unique example of folk art. It is a real community effort, as many villagers are involved in the process of creating the beautiful dressings, which are admired by thousands of visitors every year (see panel).

Tissington well dressing

Castleton Garland ceremony

The first recorded instance of well dressing was at Tissington in 1758, when the pure water supplies from the village springs was said to have spared them from the ravages of the Black Death. Another time-honoured custom takes place in the tiny chapel of Macclesfield Forest, where the rushbearing recalls the days when rushes or grasses were the only form of covering on the floors of village churches.

Just as ancient and even more mysterious is Castleton's famous Garland ceremony, held every year on 29 May, Oak Apple Day. A 'king' processes around the village on horseback, covered from head to waist in a huge 'garland' of flowers, which is later hoisted to the top of the tower of the parish church, where it is left to wither and die. Like well dressing, the custom is thought to have pagan origins, as the community welcomes the arrival of spring after the long, hard winter.

Ashbourne's rumbustious Shrovetide football game takes over the whole town, as the 'Up'ards' and the 'Down'ards' fight to score in goals which are 3 miles apart. Some experts believe that this was how the game of association football originated.

Macclesfield Forest chapel

Ashbourne Shrovetide football game

Another Shrovetide event is pancake racing through the village street of Winster, near Bakewell.

And at the other end of the year in many Peakland villages, traditional, locally composed carols are still sung every Christmastide, not in the village churches but in private houses and pubs. This custom, in which each village has its own carols, is believed to go back to the psalmodies of the Georgian period.

Among the many myths and legends which are still retained in the Peak District are many associated with the Green Man, the spirit of the woods. The many Robin Hood place-names throughout the district recall the exploits of the legendary outlaw; his faithful lieutenant, Little John, is claimed to have hailed from the Hope Valley village of Hathersage, where his grave is still pointed out between two venerable, clipped yews in the churchyard.

Also associated with the Green Man is the legend of Sir Gawain and the Green Knight, the subject of one of the earliest poems in the English language. The scene of Gawain's final, fateful encounter with the Green Knight has been identified as the secret chasm of Lud's Church, deep in the oaks of Back Forest, north of the Roaches in the Staffordshire Moorlands.

Is this the face of the Green Knight in Lud's Church?

STEP-BY-STEP GUIDE TO WELL DRESSING

Step 1: The dressing is designed, usually with a Christian theme, and traced onto paper ready for 'pricking out' in the clay.

Step 2: Villagers scour the surrounding countryside for seeds, flowers, lichens and other natural materials for the dressing.

Step 3: The wooden boards which frame the dressing are soaked for several days in the local river or stream, to ensure they retain moisture.

Step 4: The wet clay is 'puddled,' usually by trampling by foot, to make it pliable and sticky, ready to take the petals.

Step 5: The clay is then pressed firmly into place in the boards and smoothed over to create a good, even surface.

Step 6: Now the paper template of the design is 'pricked out' onto the wet clay, using a pin wheel or other sharp instrument.

Step 7: The next stage is to outline the design in the clay using black alder cones, seeds or wool, so that petalling can start.

Step 8: The real art of a well dressing is in the petalling, as villagers carefully press down flower petals, mosses, lichens, grass and rushes to colour in and shade the design.

Step 9: Finally, the boards are erected near the village well, spring or pump, roped off and decorated to stand for about a week and be admired by thousands of visitors.

Detail of well dressing

A Taste of the Peak

At one time, everywhere in Britain had its own distinctive locally produced food and drink, but in today's supermarket culture it has become increasingly difficult to find truly local products.

The Peak District is a welcome exception. Few places in Britain have such a variety of local foodstuffs and drinks, making a visit the chance to get a real 'taste of the Peak'.

Local Peak District food products

And it's not just food and drink which has the distinctive Peak District label. Encouraged by groups like Peak District Products, now entering its second decade, local craftspeople have banded together to produce a unique Peak District brand, ensuring the highest quality of craftsmanship in all their products.

These include artists and craftspeople who range from nationally known artists in watercolour and oil, to potters, woodcarvers, furniture makers and silversmiths. All obtain their inspiration from the wonderful landscapes of the Peak District, and most of the craftspeople use local materials to achieve their finished products.

Mention Peak District food to most people and they will probably come up with the name of the Bakewell tart. But don't make the mistake of calling the delicious, almond-paste and puff pastry delicacy a 'tart' in Bakewell. Here, they are known by their proper title of Bakewell puddings – and a pudding is exactly what they are. Made and sold in three or four shops in the ancient old market town on the River Wye, they are now exported all over the world.

Another unique Peak District confectionary is Ashbourne gingerbread, traditionally made in the shape of a man, just like in the fairytale, in the old market town at the gateway to Dovedale. Ashbourne also has its own special brand of mineral water taken from the crystal-clear springs which rise near the town, and now sold all over the country.

Every county once had its local cheeses, and the Peak District is fortunate to have retained the right to produce what is sometimes known as 'the king of English cheeses' – the slightly-salty, blue-veined Stilton. Real Stilton cheese is only permitted to be made in the counties of Derbyshire, Nottinghamshire and Leicestershire, and the Dairy Crest factory on the banks of the River Dove at

Farmers' market shop, Bakewell

Dairy farmer, near Ilam

Hartington, near the border with Staffordshire, just qualifies. It is sold at the specialist cheese shop in the village and at many other outlets, alongside newer local varieties such as the Buxton Blue, perhaps best enjoyed with a locally-made Derbyshire or Staffordshire oatcake.

Farmers' markets, selling wholesome locally grown and organic produce and meat, are held regularly at Ashbourne, Bakewell, Buxton, Glossop and Wirksworth. Here you can be guaranteed of fresh, locally produced meat and vegetables, in addition to cheeses, honey and preserves, and many local handmade craft items. Farm shops, such as those at Bakewell and at Pilsley on the Chatsworth Estate, and local butchers, who pride themselves in being a cut above the supermarket meat counters, are still commonplace in the Peak District.

And while staying at many Peak District bed and breakfasts, you are likely to be treated to locally produced sausage, bacon and eggs. Many local farmers are diversifying, some even making ready-made meals using local produce for the freezers in self-catering accommodation.

The pure water which rises from deep within the limestone bedrock of the Peak District is now enjoyed by people all over the world. The bottling of the previously mentioned Ashbourne, Buxton and Wildboarclough water is now a big industry, and the latest outlet for Buxton Water is seen by millions every year by the umpire's chair at the Wimbledon Lawn Tennis Championships.

A RECIPE FOR BAKEWELL PUDDING

Ingredients:

5 egg yolks	*3 egg whites*
6oz castor sugar	*4oz butter*
Essence of almond	*Strawberry jam*

Method:

1. Line a round or oval baking tin with puff pastry.
2. Melt the butter and sugar together, stir in the egg yolks and whites and the almond essence.
3. Cover the bottom of the pastry-lined tin with jam and then add the egg mixture on top.
4. Put in a hot (450° F, gas mark 7) oven for about 15 minutes, followed by a medium (350° F, gas mark 4) oven for about 30 minutes.

THE GREAT ESCAPE

It has been claimed that on any day of the year, there are likely to be more people out walking, climbing and cycling in the Peak District than anywhere else in Britain.

The reasons are easy to find. The Peak District is so accessible – half the population of England lives within 60 miles of the National Park boundary – and nowhere else has the same magical mixture of challenging rock faces, easy riverside paths through delightful dales, or testing walking or riding across wild moorland, all within such a small compass. Broadcaster and conservationist Brian Redhead, a Peak District resident himself, coined the phrase 'The Great Escape' for the Peak District, and it has certainly proved to be exactly that for the millions of people who live and work in the surrounding industrial towns and cities of the north.

Walkers on Chrome Hill

The lure of the moors, which could often be seen as a distant blue outline from their back-to-back terraced homes, was a powerful magnet to those 'ramblers from Manchester way'. But for many years, these tempting wild places on their doorsteps were agonisingly out of reach – so near yet so far away. Easily accessible for a sixpenny bus or train ride, these once common lands were barred to walkers by the grouse-shooting landlords who had acquired them during the Enclosure Movement.

Things came to a head in 1932, with the famous Mass Trespass on the western slopes of Kinder Scout, at 2088ft (636m), the highest point of the Peak District (see box).

Long-distance Paths

Britain's toughest long-distance path – the 270-mile Pennine Way – starts or finishes at Edale (depending on which way you walk it), in the shadow of the highest point of Kinder Scout. Also just about to open is a parallel multi-use trail, the 205-mile Pennine Bridleway, designed for walkers, horse-riders or cyclists, which starts from Carsington Reservoir and skirts the western edge of the Peak on its way north to Kirkby Stephen.

Other popular long-distance routes include the 50-mile Limestone Way between Matlock and Castleton, and the Gritstone Trail, 35 miles from Kidsgrove to Lyme Park, near Stockport. Other multi-use routes include the railway trails – the High Peak, Tissington and Monsal Trails and the Manifold Track – all of which pass through some of the most spectacular White Peak scenery and follow the easy gradients and curves of former railway tracks.

Other walking

Even before the CROW Act comes into force, there are over 80 square miles of Peak District moorland which are subject to access agreements with the National Park Authority where the

Heather moors at Ramshaw Rocks with Hen Cloud in the distance

walker can wander at will. These agreements cover the main moorland masses of Kinder Scout, Bleaklow, Black Hill and the Eastern Moors.

Easier walking is to be found along the escarpments of the 'edges' such as Froggatt, Curbar and Stanage, or along the cliffs of the Roaches and Hen Cloud in the west.

Easier still are the riverside paths which thread the limestone dales with Dovedale, the Manifold Valley or Lathkill Dale among the most popular.

Cycling and riding

As already described, the railway trails such as the Tissington, High Peak and Manifold, are very popular for family cycling expeditions, and with cycle-hire centres placed at strategic points you don't even have to bring your own bike (although you can if you prefer it). There are other cycle-hire centres at Fairholmes in the Upper Derwent Valley and at Carsington Reservoir. Tougher routes suitable for mountain-bikers and horse-riders are provided by the extensive network of ancient bridleways and packhorse routes which criss-cross the Peak District.

Clapper bridge across the River Bradford near Youlgreave

57

Climbing

The so-called 'working class revolution' in the until-then exclusive sport of rock-climbing took place in the 1950s on the gritstone crags and edges of the Peak District. Climbers Joe Brown and Don Whillans, Manchester plumbers both, used their mothers' clothes lines for ropes as they pushed the limits of rock climbing to new heights of skill and expertise. Crags on the Eastern Edges above the River Derwent, such as Stanage, Froggatt and Curbar and the short steep routes on the Staffordshire Roaches, still provide climbs which test the best among modern climbers.

Even harder and more sustained climbing is to be found on the massive riverside limestone crags like High Tor at Matlock Bath and Chee Tor and the charmingly-named Water-cum-Jolly on the River Wye. Peakland grit and limestone are still the test pieces for any aspiring rock jock, and many of Britain's top international climbers first cut their climbing teeth here.

Climbing at Higger Tor

Caving

Some of Britain's deepest and longest caving routes, going well beyond the famous show caves of Castleton, are found at the head of the Hope Valley, where the limestone meets the grit. Other caves are found in the sides of some of the limestone dales, such as at Stoney Middleton or Matlock Bath, and there is a flourishing branch of caving which explores the many old lead mining shafts and adits of the White Peak.

Fishing

Some would say that the popular modern sport of angling was born in the Peak District. The seventeenth-century classic *The Compleat Angler* was written here by

Fishing on Ladybower Reservoir

Izaak Walton and Charles Cotton, and some of the finest coarse fishing is still to be found on the Dove, Wye and Derwent, in addition to boat fishing on many of the reservoirs, such as Ladybower and Carsington.

Water sports

If you prefer the wind in your sails, there are yachting facilities in the thriving clubs which are situated on the reservoirs at Carsington, Errwood, Dove Stone and Torside.

Air sports

Air sports are catered for with gliding from one of the most spectacular and oldest sites in the country at Hucklow Edge, where the Derbyshire and Lancashire Gliding Club has its headquarters. Hang-gliding or parascending can be practised from many of the edges and at places such as Mam Tor in the Hope Valley and the Roaches and Morridge in Staffordshire.

Hang-glider, Eastern Edges

FORGIVE US OUR TRESPASSERS

What many people believe was the turning point of the long-running campaign for access to mountain and moorland and the creation of National Parks took place in the quiet village of Hayfield on 24 April 1932. After a well-publicised Mass Trespass on the forbidden moorland of Kinder Scout, six ramblers were arrested and five were later imprisoned merely for exercising their cherished 'right to roam.'

Initially opposed by the official ramblers' federations, the event and particularly the severity of the sentences united the walkers' cause, and finally led to National Park legislation in 1949.

The Rambler Inn at Edale

Wonders of the Age

When the first real tourists came to the Peak District in the eighteenth century, they were encouraged to take the 'Grand Tour' which showed them the so-called Seven Wonders of the Peak, a reflection of the Seven Wonders of the Ancient World.

Popularised first by Thomas Hobbes and later by Charles Cotton, they were: Peak Cavern and Mam Tor near Castleton; Poole's Hole and St Anne's Well at Buxton; Eldon Hole, Peak Forest; the Ebbing and Flowing Well at Barmoor Clough, and Chatsworth House. Many are still available as attractions for today's visitor, but there are many other 'rainy-day' alternatives to outdoor activities in the Peak.

Historic houses

Magnificent **Chatsworth House**, the Duke of Devonshire's 'Palace of the Peak', remains one of Britain's greatest showplace stately homes. This vast treasure-house of works of art from around the world is housed in a magnificent seventeenth-century Palladian house set among superb gardens and Capability Brown's renowned landscaped parkland on the banks of the River Derwent near Bakewell.

Just over the hill and often described as 'England's most perfectly-preserved medieval house' is the Duke of Rutland's **Haddon Hall**, romantically sited on a limestone bluff overlooking the banks of the River Wye. Haddon's beautiful gardens are a riot of colourful roses and other traditional garden flowers in the summer.

Haddon has often been used as a film set, as has **Lyme Park**, the seventeenth-century Palladian home of the Legh family, just outside Stockport on the western side of the Peak District. Bess of Hardwick's **Hardwick Hall** (National Trust) – 'more glass than wall' in the local saying – stands just across the M1 motorway to the east of Chesterfield.

Chatsworth

Haddon Hall

A number of smaller, more intimate country houses are also now open to the public in the Peak District. They include the Jacobean **Tissington Hall** in the village of the same name, also famous for its well dressing, and **Eyam Hall**, a splendid seventeeth-century country house which has been home to the Wright family for three centuries.

Ancient sites

High on the impressive crag above Peak Cavern at Castleton stands the Peak District's most impressive medieval monument, the romantic ruins of the eleventh-century **Peveril Castle**, now in the care of English Heritage. **Bolsover Castle** (also English Heritage) belongs to another era when castles were being converted to stately country houses, although it stands on the site of another of the Peverils' fortresses. Older still are the prehistoric stone circles of **Arbor Low**, near Monyash and **Nine Ladies** on Stanton Moor, near Bakewell.

Show caves

Two more of the original Wonders are today show caverns welcoming thousands of visitors every year. The great yawning mouth of **Peak Cavern** (which recently reverted to its old name of 'Devil's Arse') is said to be the biggest cave entrance in Britain and houses the remains of recently restored rope-making works. Mary Queen of Scots was one of the earliest visitors to **Poole's Cavern** at Buxton, where 20 shallow steps make the underground wonders accessible to all ages and abilities.

Both the **Treak Cliff** and **Blue John Caverns** at Castleton show examples of the unique, semi-precious banded fluorspar known as Blue John, and at Treak Cliff you can see where it is made

Entrance to Peak Cavern

into dishes and jewellery. At **Speedwell Cavern** under Mam Tor you have to take a 200-metre boat trip along an underground canal cut by former lead miners to reach the destination of the 'Bottomless Pit'. In contrast, the **Great Masson** and **Great**

Rutland Caverns at Matlock Bath are usually reached by an exciting **cable car** ride to the **Heights of Abraham** (see page 66).

Museums and heritage centres

Still on the underground theme, the **Peak District Mining Museum** and **Temple Mine** below the Heights of Abraham transport the visitor back to the days of lead mining and close by is the **Matlock Bath Aquarium.**

Other Peak District museums include Buxton's **Art Gallery and Museum**, with its fascinating displays of Peak District history and 'Wonders of the Peak' display, and the **Old House Museum** in Bakewell – claimed to be the oldest tax collector's house in the Peak. The award-winning **Eyam Museum** vividly describes the story of the tragic 'visitation' of the plague in 1665–66.

Millennium Bridge at New Mills

Wirksworth's fascinating **Heritage Centre** tells the story of this town in the heart of lead mining country, and the **National Stone Centre** just outside the town, graphically reveals the history of Peak District stone and its many and various uses. The **New Mills Heritage Centre** stands above the dizzying **Torrs Millennium Walkway** over the River Goyt. You can see where the career of James Brindley, 'the father of England's canals', started at the **Brindley Mill Museum** in Leek, while nearby at the **Cheddleton Flint Mill**, the story of how flint was processed to make pottery at nearby Stoke-on-Trent is graphically told.

When Richard Arkwright set up the first water-powered cotton mill in the world at Cromford in 1771, the Derwent Valley became a cradle of the Industrial Revolution, a fact which recently received international recognition by its designation as a World Heritage Site. The **Derwent Valley Visitor Centre** at Belper and **Masson Mill** at Cromford both have fascinating museums illustrating the industrial heritage of the valley.

Theme and Country Parks

Britain's premier theme park **Alton Towers,** near Uttoxeter, offers children of all ages the chance to experience breathtaking white-knuckle rides such as Oblivion, Nemesis and the latest stomach-churner which is known as Air. Also perfect for a rainy-day

Heights of Abraham cable cars

excursion is the **Gulliver's Kingdom** theme park at Matlock Bath, and the **cable car** which will take you high above the River Derwent to the **Heights of Abraham**.

Thomas the Tank Engine is a regular visitor to the **Peak Rail** headquarters at Matlock, and steam trains can be taken along the old Midland Line as far as Rowsley, and also along the beautiful **Churnet Valley Railway** in Staffordshire. Slighty further away is the award-winning **Magna** science adventure centre at Templeborough, Rotherham.

Country Parks, with picnic tables and other facilities can be found at **Carsington, Trentabank** and **Tittesworth** reservoirs, as well as at **Longshaw, Buxton** and **Ilam Hall.**

Gardens and zoos

Gardeners will delight in the **Lea Rhododendron Gardens** near Matlock; the **Dunge Valley Hidden Gardens**, near Kettleshulme, and the horticultural tour of the world which can be undertaken at the **Biddulph Grange Gardens** in Staffordshire.

But if animals are your fascination, then visit the **Chestnut Centre**, near Chapel-en-le-Frith, where rare native creatures like otters can be seen close at hand. The **Blackbrook Zoological Park** and **Churnet Valley Wildlife Park** both have many examples of rare and unusual animals on show, while the **Freshfields Donkey Village** at Peak Forest rescues mistreated donkeys.

TOP TEN STATELY HOMES

Bolsover Castle (NT)

Chatsworth, near Bakewell

Calke Abbey (NT)

Eyam Hall

Haddon Hall, near Bakewell

Hardwick Hall (NT), near Chesterfield

Ilam Hall (NT)

Lyme Park (NT), Stockport

Sudbury Hall (NT), near Ashbourne

Tissington Hall

A Peak District Gazetteer

Ashbourne

Dubbed 'the Gateway to Dovedale', the pleasant, largely Georgian, market town of Ashbourne boasts one of the finest parish churches in the Peak, and one of its oldest schools. The soaring spire of the mainly thirteenth-century church of St Oswald dominates the lower part of the town, where the Old Grammar School, founded in 1585, faces St John's Street. Ashbourne is also the southern terminus of the Tissington Trail.

Ashbourne

Old Grammar School, Ashbourne

Ashford-in-the-Water

The Sheepwash Bridge which spans the River Wye at Ashford has been the subject of countless paintings and photographs. And the village itself, consisting substantially of eighteenth-century cottages, is a candidate for one of the prettiest in the Peak. It dresses six wells in early June.

Ashford-in-the-Water

Bakewell

There has been a settlement at Bakewell for at least 1000 years, and it is the largest village (pop. 4000) within the area of the National Park. Bakewell still holds the major agricultural market for the area every Monday in the modern Agricultural Business Centre, and the headquarters of the National Park authority is on the Baslow Road. The charming fourteenth-century Town Bridge leads past the gabled, seventeenth-century Old Market Hall, now a Tourist Information Centre, into Rutland Square. The Old House Museum in Cunningham Place is appropriately found in what is thought to be the oldest house in Bakewell. This is also home of the famous Bakewell Pudding.

Bakewell

Bath Gardens, Bakewell

Bamford

This small village beneath the frowning crags of Bamford Edge is perhaps best known for its church of St John the Baptist, where the dead from the reservoir-threatened villages of Derwent and Ashopton were reinterred, with a suitable memorial, in the churchyard. Bamford Mill, built to spin cotton in 1820, now provides high-class accommodation for commuters to Sheffield.

Bradfield, Upper and Lower

The two Bradfields are tucked away in the upper reaches of the Loxley Valley to the west of Sheffield. Little-visited, they are two of the prettiest villages in the Peak, and Upper Bradfield's parish church of St Nicholas is one of the finest-sited. The Watch House at the entrance to the churchyard was built to deter body-snatchers.

Buxton

The elegant market town of Buxton, standing at over 1000 feet above the sea, was only excluded from the Peak District National Park because of the huge limestone quarries which surround it. In many ways, it is the cultural capital of the Peak, with

The Crescent, Buxton

the stunning Georgian architecture of The Crescent; the enormous dome of the Great Stables, latterly the Devonshire Hospital (recently acquired by the University of Derby), and the Victorian splendour of the Pavilion and Pavilion Gardens. Frank Matcham's exuberant rococo masterpiece of the Opera House is now the home of the annual Buxton Festival of the Music and Arts, and is known as 'the theatre in the hills'. The discovery by the Romans of Buxton's natural mineral springs laid the foundation of its fame and, in the eighteenth century, the 5th Duke of Devonshire expended vast sums on The Crescent and Great Stables in an effort to make the town a spa to rival Bath or Cheltenham.

Castleton

There are many attractions for visitors in this tiny medieval village which stands at the head of the Hope Valley. The show caverns of Peak, Treak Cliff, Blue John and Speedwell all offer different aspects of the Peak's underground riches, while the ruins of Peveril Castle (English Heritage), on the crag above Peak Cavern, is the finest medieval monument in the district. Castleton's Christmas lights are justly famous, and many shops sell examples of Castleton's unique semi-precious gemstone, Blue John. Nearby is the spectacular Winnats Pass, and the 'Shivering Mountain' of Mam Tor.

Chapel-en-le-Frith

Chapel-en-le-Frith was founded in medieval times as 'the chapel in the forest' – the Royal Forest of the Peak. Clustered around its ancient market-place, complete with cross and stocks, Chapel's cobbled streets and winding alleys has a special charm, missed by many visitors. The parish church of St Thomas à Becket is a little Georgian gem just off the market-place.

Chesterfield

The famous twisted spire of thirteenth-century St Mary and All Saints parish church is thought to have been caused by the use of unseasoned timber beneath the lead cladding of the exterior. The church itself is almost cathedral-like in its proportions, and houses impressive tombs to the local Foljambe family. Chesterfield is chiefly an

Chesterfield

industrial town, founded on its engineering works and the nearby North Derbyshire coalfield. It centres on its extensive cobbled market-place, which won a Casa Nostra award for its sensitive and imaginative redevelopment.

Cromford

Cromford is inextricably linked with Richard Arkwright and the first rumblings of the Industrial Revolution. It was here at the Old Mill in 1771 that Arkwright was the first to harness the power of the streams feeding into the River Derwent to power his cotton factory. Later, he was to develop Cromford into one of the earliest model villages, and the influence of his benefaction can be seen everywhere, from the sturdy cottages he built for his workers on Cromford Hill and North Street, to the dignified buildings surrounding Greyhound Square. Cromford is the centrepiece of the new Derwent Valley World Heritage Site.

Edale

Walkers will know Edale as the southern terminus of the 270-mile Pennine Way, the first and toughest of Britain's national trails. Situated at the foot of Kinder Scout, at 2088ft (636m) the highest point of the Peak District, Edale village is more properly known as Grindsbrook Booth, Edale being the name of the valley of the River Noe.

Edale

Eyam

It was the arrival of the plague in 1665–66 which really put Eyam on the map, and thousands of visitors still come to marvel at the unselfish sacrifice made by the villagers as they quarantined themselves in an attempt to halt the spread of the dread disease to neighbouring villages. There are touching memorials throughout the village and in the parish church to those who died, and the excellent Eyam Museum tells the story of the terrible events of three centuries ago. Eyam Hall (open to the public) has been in the Wright family for 300 years.

Eyam church sundial

Eyam Plague Cottages

Glossop

A former mill and factory town on the western edge of the Peak District, Glossop retains an air of bustling importance, especially around The Square in the centre of town. Glossop gained its industrial importance largely through the efforts of the Howard family, Dukes of Norfolk. The industrial quarter is still known as Howard Town, and their coat of arms is seen everywhere. The old market town was centred on Old Glossop, where seventeenth-century cottages cluster around the parish church of All Saints.

Grindleford

Situated on an important crossing of the mighty River Derwent, Grindleford probably gets its name from the grind-stones which were quarried from nearby Froggatt Edge. Close by are the oak woods of Padley Gorge (NT) and Padley Chapel, an important Roman Catholic shrine to two dissenters who were taken from there and executed in the Armada year of 1588.

Hartington

The Dairy Crest Cheese Factory just off the village square at Hartington is where the famous Hartington Stilton cheese is made, and sold in the local specialist

Padley Chapel

Hartington

Hartington village pond

cheese shop. The village is centred on the square with its restored mere (pond), and is a convenient centre for exploring the Dove Valley. Tudor Hartington Hall, just outside the village, is allegedly the place where Bonnie Prince Charles stayed on his ill-fated march on London in 1645, and is now a recently restored youth hostel.

Hathersage

The name may mean 'heather ridge,' an apt description of the moorland slopes which lead up to the climbers' Mecca of Stanage Edge, above the village. Once the centre of a flourishing millstone and nail, pin and needle-making industry, Hathersage has today become something of a commuter village to nearby Sheffield. The church, which dates from the four-teenth century, is noted for its fine brasses and the 'grave' of Little John in the church-yard. Nearby is the fine Elizabethan towerhouse of North Lees Hall.

Little John's grave at Hathersage churchyard

Hayfield

A pleasant market town, founded on former wool, cotton, paper and textile printing mills, which utilised the power of the Rivers Sett and Kinder flowing down from the western flanks of Kinder Scout, which dominate the village. Hayfield was the starting point of the 1932 Kinder Scout Mass Trespass, which is commemorated by a plaque at Bowden Bridge Quarry car park, on the Kinder Road.

Holmfirth

For ever now associated with the long-running television comedy *Last of the Summer Wine*, which has been shot here for over thirty years, Holmfirth has many other attractions, including its unique postcard museum. Nearby is the Holme Moss BBC TV transmitter on Black Hill.

Langsett

A gateway village to the Peak District from the northeast, Langsett suffers somewhat from the busy A616 trunk road which thunders through it. But there are some splendid walks from the Langsett Barn car park, around the reservoir or further west across the Langsett and Midhope Moors into the Derwent Valley.

Leek

Leek is the capital of the Staffordshire Moorlands, a town centred on its cobbled market-place and famous for its former silk and cotton factories, heavily supported by William Morris of the Arts & Crafts movement. Today it is perhaps best known for its large number and great variety of of antique shops. Brindley Mill, built by the canal pioneer James Brindley, is now a museum to his memory and nearby on the River Churnet is the Cheddleton Flint Mill, where flint was ground for use in the Potteries, and the Churnet Valley Railway.

Longnor

On the ridge which separates the Dove and Manifold Valleys, Longnor is a moorland market town which was once more important than nearby Buxton. The scale of charges on the old Market Hall (now a craft centre) in the cobbled village square gives an indication of its former importance and prosperity, while the village itself is an ideal centre for the exploration of the little-known Staffordshire moorlands and the Upper Dove Valley. It is also the real-life location for TV's long-running medical drama *Peak Practice*.

Great & Little Longstone

The twin villages of the Longstones lie at the foot of Longstone Edge, a limestone ridge which is riddled with old lead mines, leading up to Monsal Dale.

Great Longstone

Historically, the villagers existed on the traditional dual economy of the Peak District – lead mining and farming – but another important industry of Great Longstone was boot and shoemaking. This is reflected in the name of one of the village pubs, the Crispin after the patron saint of shoemakers and cobblers.

Macclesfield

It's no coincidence that Macclesfield's inner ring road is known as 'The Silk Road,' nor its football team as the 'Silkmen'. During the eighteenth and nineteenth centuries, it gradually replaced Derby as the centre for the silk manufacturing trade, and the story of the growth of the industry is graphically told in the Silk Museum and Paradise Mill at the Heritage Centre in Roe Street, where you can still see Jacquard handloom weaving taking place. The town is convenient for exploring Macclesfield Forest and the western edge of the Peak.

Matlock

The administrative capital of Derbyshire, Matlock is a bustling Derwent-side town which was created by the gradual merger of no less than eight hamlets. When John Smedley built his Hydro there in 1853, it became for a short period a spa town to rival Buxton in its heyday. The huge Hydro building still dominates the town, and is now the headquarters of Derbyshire County Council. Gone now is the Bank Road cable-hauled tramway, said to be the steepest in the world until it closed in 1927. On the hill above, backing every view, is the gaunt shell of John Smedley's Riber Castle, never completed and still in search of a new use.

Matlock Bath

Once known as Little Switzerland because of its position in the deep gorge of the Derwent, Matlock Bath came into its own as a tourist destination with the coming of the Midland Railway in 1849. Joseph Paxton's Swiss chalet-style railway station now serves as the Whistlestop Centre of the Derbyshire Wildlife Trust. Modern attractions include the Great Rutland and Masson Caverns, the Peak District Mining Museum in the Pavilion, and Gulliver's Kingdom, a children's theme park. The Heights of Abraham, on the hillside opposite High Tor, are usually reached today by cable car, yet another echo of the Alps and Switzerland.

New Mills

One of the Peak District's most exciting new attractions is the Millennium Walkway which runs high above the rushing waters of the River Goyt in the riverside park known as The Torrs at New Mills. You get a close-up aerial view of the 'new mills' after which the town was named from this elevated, stainless steel walkway which has been engineered into the side of a vertical stone embankment. There's an excellent Heritage Centre in the town.

Stoney Middleton

The Roman Baths pointed out to visitors in The Nook at Stoney Middleton are certainly not Roman, but built on the site of warm springs by one of the village's most distinguished residents, Lord Denman, a Victorian Lord Chief Justice. Stoney is squeezed comfortably between the high limestone crags of Middleton Dale, a popular venue for modern rock climbers. The parish church of St Martin is unusual for its octagonal nave.

Tideswell

Forever associated with its magnificent parish church of St John the Baptist – the so-called 'Cathedral of the Peak' – Tideswell lay at the centre of the Royal Forest of the Peak where medieval kings and princes hunted game. Later, sheep farming and lead mining became the village trades, and it was from the riches won from this traditional dual economy that the beautiful parish church was built. Constructed within the remark-

Tideswell

ably short period of only seventy years, St John's is almost exclusively in the light and airy Decorated style, best seen in the chancel. The pinnacled tower was added in the Perpendicular style later.

Tissington

No less than five well dressings are held at Ascensiontide in the pretty limestone village of Tissington, where the custom was first recorded in 1758. The village is dominated by two buildings, the stately, eighteenth-century mansion of Tissington Hall, home of the Fitzherbert family for four centuries and recently

Tissington

opened to the public, and the squat Norman tower of the parish church of St Mary, on the hill opposite.

Warslow

Formerly an estate village owned by the Harpur Crewe family, Warslow is a good centre for exploring the Staffordshire moors. The Victorian church, built by Sir George Crewe, features beautiful examples of early-twentieth-century glass by William Morris and Company. He also built Warslow Hall on the Longnor Road as a shooting lodge.

Whaley Bridge

Whaley Bridge, a formerly industrial mill town on the western side of the Peak, is a convenient centre for exploring the beautiful Goyt Valley, with its twin reservoirs of Errwood and Fernilee, just to the south. The Peak Forest Canal, later linked to the Cromford Canal by the Cromford and High Peak Railway (now the High Peak Trail) has a terminus here, and is now once again very popular with narrow-boat owners.

Wirksworth

Wirksworth was built on stone, and is still surrounded by limestone quarries, one of which has been converted to become the National Stone Centre, just outside the town. The Moot Hall in Chapel Lane is the only surviving specialist building for the lead miners' Barmote Court, one of the most ancient in the country. The parish church of St Mary is one of the most interesting in the Peak and stands in

Wirksworth

a cathedral-like close just off the sloping, cobbled market place. Its chief glories are an intricately carved Saxon coffin lid dating from around 800, and the charming, apparently skirted figure of 't'owd man' – the local name for a lead miner.

Youlgreave

The splendid Perpendicular tower of Youlgreave's parish church of All Saints dominates this busy, linear village, which stands high above Bradford Dale. Below the church in the main street stands The Fountain, dated 1829, which is a reminder that the village has its own private water supply, even today. Nearly opposite is the former Cooperative Shop, now one of the most unusual youth hostels in the Peak District.

TAKE A BREAK FROM THE CAR

Unlike many rural areas, the Peak District is blessed with an extensive network of public transport routes, making it easier than most other places for you to enjoy the beautiful countryside – and leave the car at home. In fact, one of the best ways to enjoy the Peak District is to hop on a bus or train and leave your car – as well as your cares – behind.

By leaving your car at home you will be doing your bit by contributing to the protection and enhancement of this precious landscape. You will be able to sit back and enjoy the wonderful landscapes of the Peak District without worrying about traffic queues or finding somewhere to park.

And by leaving the car behind, you will be making a direct and positive contribution to the environment by reducing traffic congestion and air pollution in the National Park and surrounding area. Precious time will also be saved in not having to search for somewhere to park – and you will also, of course, save the expense of parking fees.

More and more people are taking advantage of the excellent train and bus services which criss-cross the Peak District area. Walkers, in particular, are finding that they can do longer, linear walks, using public transport, without the need to do circular routes which start and finish at your car-parking place. The Hope Valley railway line is a good example of where this can be achieved in spectacular walking country.

Also available in good walking country are the Park 'n' Ride services which have been provided in the Upper Derwent Valley and at the Roaches in Staffordshire in order to combat severe road congestion in these popular areas. The Upper Derwent Service runs throughout the summer and at winter weekends from the Fairholmes Visitor Centre, where there is also a cycle-hire centre, and the Roaches service runs from Severn-Trent's Tittesworth Reservoir, just outside the National Park.

The Peak District's buses and trains offer an all-year-round service, and most run daily. And in the Staffordshire Moorlands area a Post Bus delivers both the mail and passengers on a circular route from Monday to Saturday, connecting Leek with a number of remote villages in the Peak District, including Warslow, Hartington and Alstonefield. The Moorlands Traveller also operates an on-demand service six days a week which provides a fixed-fare, door-to-door service which is wheelchair-friendly.

In addition, there are special day runabout tickets which enable you to use the services of different bus or train companies, without the hassle of bothering with separate fares. These include:

Derbyshire Wayfarer. This covers most Peak District bus and rail services, plus the whole of the rest of Derbyshire. It also allows for direct links to Sheffield, Leek and Macclesfield.

Family Freedom. This covers the Sunday Peak Bus Network, as marketed by Derbyshire County Council. It gives unlimited travel for a day for up to two adults and three children.

Greater Manchester Wayfarer. This also covers most Peak District bus and train services, as well as the whole of Greater Manchester, including Metrolink.

Hope Valley Family Freedom. This service covers the Sunday Peak Bus Network in the Hope Valley, excluding the Hope Valley line train service.

South Yorkshire Peak Explorer. This covers all bus and train services in South Yorkshire and buses into the Peak District from Sheffield as far as Bakewell, Buxton and Glossop.

In addition, individual operators also operate daily network tickets, including: **Stagecoach East Midlands Day Rover.** Available every day on Stagecoach's routes in the East Midlands, and

Trent Zig Zag Plus. A daily ticket covering all Trent's bus services.

Full details and information on services and fares can be obtained at travel centres, bus and railway stations and information centres in and around the Peak District.

Publications

Essential reading for anyone using public transport to explore Derbyshire and the Peak District National Park is the comprehensive *Peak District Timetable*, published by Derbyshire County Council, which gives details of all bus and train times in the area. It costs 60p or £1.20 by post from Derbyshire County Council's Public Transport Unit, County Hall, Smedley Street, Matlock, Derbyshire DE4 2AG.

Access for All is a free guide for people with disabilities who are considering a visit to the Peak District. It includes public transport information and is available from the Peak District National Park Authority on 01629 816200.

The Hope Valley Leisure Guide is another free guide which covers the scenic Hope Valley, and includes bus and train times and information about local attractions and activities and special events, such as guided walks and the special Jazz and Folk Trains on the Hope Valley line. For your copy, write to the Hope Valley & High Peak Transport Partnership, c/o The Town Hall, New Mills, High Peak SK22 4AT, or call the Events Line on 0161 242 6296.

Travel Helplines

Traveline (buses throughout the UK)	0870 608 2608
National Rail Enquiries	0845 748 4950
National Express	0870 580 8080
Tripscope (travel advice for people with disabilities)	0845 758 5641
First North Western (rail travel for people with disabilities)	0845 760 40231
Hope Valley line (events)	0161 242 6296
Post Bus (from Leek)	01538 382372
Moorlands Traveller (Staffordshire Moorlands)	01538 386888

Useful websites

Traveline	www.traveline.org.uk
Derbyshire	www.derbysbus.net
Rail journey planner	www.thetrainline.com
Railtrack	www.railtrack.co.uk
Taxies from stations	www.traintaxi.com
National Express	www.gobycoach.com

USEFUL ADDRESSES

Peak District National Park Authority
Aldern House
Baslow Road
Bakewell
Derbyshire
DE45 1AE
Tel: 01629 816200

Derbyshire Dales District Council
Town Hall
Matlock
Derbyshire
DE45 3NN
Tel: 01629 580580

High Peak Borough Council
Town Hall
Buxton
Derbyshire
SK17 6EL
Tel: 01298 23114

Staffordshire Moorlands District Council
1 Market Place
Leek
Staffordshire
ST13 5HH
Tel: 01538 483741

Heart of England Tourist Board
Larkhill Road
Worcester
WR5 2EZ
Tel: 01905 761100

Yorkshire Tourist Board
312 Tadcaster Road
York
YO24 1GS
Tel: 01904 701100

North West Tourist Board
Swan House
Swan Meadow Road
Wigan Pier
Wigan
Lancashire
WN3 5BB
Tel: 01942 821222

National Trust
East Midlands Regional Office
The Stableyard
Clumber Park
Worksop
Nottinghamshire
S80 3BE
Tel: 01909 486411

Youth Hostels Association
Trevelyan House
Dimple Road
Matlock
Derbyshire
DE4 3YH
Tel: 0870 870 8808

Friends of the Peak District
Council for the Protection of Rural England
Sheffield & Peak District Branch
22a Endcliffe Crescent
Sheffield
S10 3BE
Tel: 0114 266 5822